# Baha'i Faith

By
Oracle Claretta Pam

# Baha'i Faith

Oracle Claretta Pam

*Published and printed in the United States by Sacred Vision Press, an imprint of Innovative Publishers, Inc., a division of Global Nebula, LLC, Boston, Massachusetts.* 

**Oracle Claretta Pam**


| | |
|---|---|
| ISBN-10: 1-4913-1626-8 | ISBN-13: 978-1-4913-1626-9 Paperback |
| ISBN-10: 1-4913-1657-8 | ISBN-13: 978-1-4913-1657-3 Hardback |
| ISBN-10: 1-4913-1688-8 | ISBN-13: 978-1-4913-1688-7 Kindle |
| ISBN-10: 1-4913-1717-5 | ISBN-13: 978-1-4913-1717-4 iBook |
| ISBN-10: 1-4913-1777-9 | ISBN-13: 978-1-4913-1777-8 Nook |
| ISBN-10: 1-4913-1744-2 | ISBN-13: 978-1-4913-1744-0 AudioBook |

---

Library of Congress Cataloging-in-Publication Data

Pam, Oracle Claretta.
The Baha'i Faith / Oracle Claretta Pam. -- First edition.
pages cm
ISBN 1-4913-1626-8 (pbk. : alk. paper) -- ISBN 1-4913-1657-8 (hardback : alk. paper) -- ISBN 1-4913-1688-8 (ebook) -- ISBN 1-4913-1717-5 (ebook) -- ISBN 1-4913-1744-2 (audiobk.) -- ISBN 1-4913-1777-9 (ebook)
1. Bahai Faith. I. Title.
BP365.P36 2014
297.9'3--dc23

2014010419

***Published and printed in the United States by***
***Innovative Publishers, Inc., Boston, Massachusetts***

***10 9 8 7 6 5 4 3 2 1 14 15 16 17 18***

*Baha'i* Faith

***First edition. September 2014***

DEDICATION

To everyone and
everything in this universe.

# CONTENTS

# ACKNOWLEDGMENTS

A special note of thanks to the congregation at the Universal Life Church Monastery of Massachusetts both online and on the ground. Your encouragement and participation and spreading the understanding of all belief systems is what will effect positive change in this world and beyond.

I

# *Introduction to the Baha'i Faith*

Perhaps the youngest of the world's monotheistic religions, the *Baha'i* Faith has—since its obscure origins in the mid-nineteenth century—rapidly swept the globe, establishing itself as an independent religious ideology that constitutes one of the fastest-growing religions of today.

Despite its relatively recent emergence and its underlying parallels with the centuries-old pre-existing religions of the world, the *Baha'i* Faith has secured a distinct place in its own right as a unique and independent faith which is considered by some religious scholars to in fact possess an upper hand compared to its predecessors—particularly in terms of its recent birth. Edward Granville Browne, one of the earliest and most prominent Western historians to have studied the *Baha'i* Faith, has referred to the faith as "*a religion of modern times*" that is "*naturally more accessible for study and understanding than the older religions.*" According to Browne, the world's leading major religions of today date back hundreds and thousands of years with much of their authentic history becoming lost, rendering them largely inaccessible for study as a result. On the contrary, the *Baha'i* Faith, having originated less than two centuries ago, presents a wide array of sources and rich empirical data to researchers and historians, thus allowing them to gain a detailed insight into its origins and development.

At the same time, much like the other major religions that were born out of pre-existing faiths and influences, it would similarly also be impossible to isolate the *Baha'i* Faith from the religion that paved the way for its birth—the religion of Islam.

## 2

# *Babism* and early history

The origins of the *Baha'i* Faith can be traced back to the mid-nineteenth century CE in Iran, having essentially taken its roots from Shiite Islam. The central idea of the faith was derived from the Islamic doctrine of the *Mahdi*—"the guided one"—a messianic figure believed to be a descendent of Prophet Muhammad, who is prophesied to emerge near the end of times to revive the religion of Islam. This idea was culminated in the "*Twelver*" Shiite ideology which regards the *Mahdi* as the twelfth *Imam* (successor), descending from a series of *Imams* tracing back to Prophet Muhammad and was what ultimately formed the basis for the Baha'i Faith in the face of a religious leader named Siyyid 'Ali Mohammad Shirazi—better known to world as the *Bab*.

'Ali Mohammad was a merchant born in Shirazi, Iran. At the age of twenty-four, following a series of prophetic dreams, he claimed to be the promised *"Al-Qaim"* (*Mahdi*) in the year 1844. Despite conflicting views on the context and nature of these claims, there remains to be a general consensus on his distinctive claim to authority, which is understood to be that of the *Hidden Imam.*

Soon after his declaration, he assumed the title of the *Bab* (The Gate) and his message began to spread across Persia, gaining an ardent following that embraced his teachings and were thus labeled *Babis.* His Divinely guided verses were recorded in *Qayyumu'l-Asma'* (The Maintainer of the Divine Names)—an extensive treatise containing the *Bab's* message and claim to authority—which came to be recognized by his followers as *"the Quran of the Babis."*

It wasn't long, however, before his rising influence triggered a strong opposition from the Shiite religious clergy and the Persian government, who perceived it as a threat to their own power and position. The *Bab* was arrested and imprisoned thereafter upon orders of the governor of Shiraz and after spending several years being tortured in captivity, he was finally executed on account of heresy by a firing squad in the year 1850. A number of his adherents were also persecuted and put to death along with their leader and the *Babi* movement soon began to disintegrate with the rise of new leaders and clerics, each proposing a different set of ideas and plans of their own.

It was during this period that one of the *Bab's* earliest and most devoted disciples, Mirza Hoseyn 'Ali Nuri—known by the *Babi* title of *Baha'u'llah* (the "Glory of God")—began to gain imminence as a prominent *Babi* leader.

Following the execution of the *Bab*, a group of *Babis* in Tehran led by the *Bab's* deputy, Mullah Shaykh 'Ali Turshizi, conspired an assassination plot against the Shah, Nasser al-Din Shah Qajar, to avenge the death of *Bab*. *Baha'u'llah* strongly condemned the plot, but was unable to exercise any influence he may have had when he was exiled to Baghdad in 1851 upon instruction of the chief minister. The assassination attempt ultimately failed and all those found to be associated with the conspiracy were arrested and killed, soon igniting the outbreak of violent riots against the entire *Babi* community issued by the Shah, which resulted in the death of hundreds of *Babis*.

In the midst of the ensuing massacre, *Baha'u'llah*

was arrested and imprisoned in Tehran, where he spent four months in captivity inside an underground dungeon along with his followers, living in the most inhumane conditions. During his incarceration, *Baha'u'llah* is believed to have received a Divine revelation through a dream, declaring him the *"The Manifestation of God"*—the promised messenger whose coming had been foretold by the *Bab* in his writings, where he referred to him as *"He whom God shall make manifest"*. The *Bab* maintained that the coming of this messenger had been prophesied by previous religions before him, stating that this messianic figure would establish God's kingdom on Earth. He urged all his followers to pledge their allegiance to the *Promised One,* without revealing his name or identity, instructing them to disregard all writings after his death until the appearance of this man.

After his release from imprisonment, *Baha'u'llah* returned to Baghdad in 1853 and continued to keep his Divine revelation secret. His increasing influence in the *Babi* community, however, was met with resentment by the *Bab's* appointed leader, Mirza Yahya, eventually causing *Baha'u'llah* to leave the city in pursuit of a solitary life in the mountains of Kurdistan, where he lived for two years as an ascetic.

He initially wandered the mountains dressed as a dervish, identifying himself by the name *Darvish Muhammad-i-Irani*, which later brought him to the Sufi leaders at the regional center of Sulaymaniyyah, who began to seek his wisdom and knowledge. It was during this time that *Baha'u'llah* penned some of his most famous works of writing including *The Four Valleys*. In the year 1856, he finally returned to Baghdad upon the insistence of his family.

*Baha'u'llah* now dedicated his life to reviving the teachings of the *Bab* and regenerating the spirit of the *Babi* community, soon establishing himself as a distinguished spiritual leader in all of Persia and its neighboring countries, winning over government officials as well as the Sunni clerics.

During this period, *Baha'u'llah* wrote *Kitab-ul-Iqan* (The Book of Certitude), highlighting God's Divine plan for all of humanity, which went on to become one of his most influential writings, laying down the foundations for what was later to become the *Baha'i* Faith.

## 3

## *Baha'u'llah's* declaration and the birth of the *Baha'i* Faith

The increasing influence of *Baha'u'llah* soon began to draw the attention of the Persian government and the Islamic clergy, who in fear of his rising power, pressured the Ottoman government to extradite him to Persia. The Ottoman government, however, refused and instead transferred *Baha'u'llah* to Constantinople.

During this time, *Baha'u'llah* departed from Baghdad and settled in the Najibiyyih Garden at the Tigris River, which became his temporary abode. The garden was later renamed the Garden of *Rivdan* (Paradise) and it was here that he disclosed his identity as *"He whom God shall make manifest"*—the promised messenger whose coming had been prophesied by the *Bab*—to a handful of his close companions. *Baha'u'llah's* declaration marked the beginning of a new era for the *Babi* community and was what eventually led to the emergence of a new religion, independent of *Babism:* the *Baha'i* Faith.

The twelve days that *Baha'u'llah* spent at the Garden of *Rivdan* later came to be regarded as a period of great religious significance by the *Baha'i* community and are celebrated by them today as the festival of *Rivdan.*

On August 1863, *Baha'u'llah* arrived in Constantinople, where the Ottoman government was soon persuaded by Persian authorities to exile him and his companions to Adrianople, accusing the *Babi* community of being a threat to the Ottoman Empire.

*Baha'u'llah's* arrival in Adrianople drew a wave of new devotees whose hearts were won over by his message of peace and unity. During his stay in the city, *Baha'u'llah* reached out to his brother, Mirza Yahya, a prominent *Babi* leader at the time, to inform him of his Divine station and announce the nature of his mission. Yahya, however, following his failed attempts to have *Baha'u'llah* assassinated, responded by proclaiming himself the *Promised One* instead. He then made an open challenge to *Baha'u'llah* at a mosque, inviting him to undergo a Divine test in order to expose the imposter. *Baha'u'llah* accepted and ultimately became recognized as the undisputed *Promised One,* after Yahya's eventual refusal to show up.

It was then that the *Babis,* for the first time, began to refer to themselves as *Baha'is* and the *Baha'i* Faith was born as a distinct and independent religion.

In the year 1867, *Baha'u'llah* began to compose a series of letters addressed to *"the Kings of the Earth"*, proclaiming himself the *Promised One* whose coming had been prophesied in the sacred texts and scriptures of all religions, including Islam, Christianity and Judaism. His letters highlighted his universal message of the oneness of humanity, where he urged all world leaders to join him in the effort to establish world peace and unity. He described his message in the following words in an excerpt from one of his letters:

*"The time must come when the imperative necessity for the holding of a vast, an all-embracing assemblage of men will be universally realized. The rulers and kings of the earth must needs attend it, and, participating in its deliberations, must consider such ways and means as will lay the foundations of the world's Great Peace amongst men. Such a peace demandeth that the Great Powers should resolve, for the sake of the tranquility of the peoples of the earth, to be fully reconciled among themselves. Should any king take up arms against another, all should unitedly arise and prevent him. If this be done, the nations of the world will no longer require any armaments, except for the purpose of preserving the security of their realms and of maintaining internal order within their territories. This will ensure the peace and composure of every people, government and nation."*

—Gleanings from the Writings of *Baha'u'llah*

The public proclamation of the new faith had barely begun when Mirza Yahya denounced *Baha'u'llah's* message and attempted to discredit him to the Ottoman government. In 1868, following the resulting investigation issued by the government, the *Babis* were once more exiled and sentenced to imprisonment upon royal command. While Yahya was exiled in Cyprus along with his followers, the *Baha'is* and their leader, *Baha'u'llah,* were sent to the city of Akka (Acre). There, they were held captive for two years under harsh conditions which proved to be a period of extreme hardship and difficulty for the *Baha'i* prisoners.

The locals and officials gradually began to be moved by *Baha'u'llah's* influence, who eventually won their admiration and the governors eased the conditions of his imprisonment, ultimately allowing him to leave Akka.

Despite still being a prisoner of the Ottoman Empire, *Baha'u'llah* spent his remaining years at the Mansion of Bahji, where he devoted his time to writing. It was during this period that he composed a number of his most notable works, including the *Kitab-i-Aqdas* (The Book of Laws).

Cambridge historian and orientalist, Edward Granville Browne, met *Baha'u'llah* during his stay at the mansion in 1891 and described his experience in one of the most famous accounts of the leader:

*"The face of him on whom I gazed I can never forget, though I cannot describe it. Those piercing eyes seemed to read one's very soul; power and authority sat on that ample brow; while the deep lines on the forehead and face implied an age which the jet-black hair and beard flowing down in indistinguishable luxuriance almost to the waist seemed to belie. No need to ask in whose presence I stood, as I bowed myself before one who is the object of a devotion and love which kings might envy and emperors sigh for in vain!"*

—**Edward G. Browne,** ***"A Traveler's Narrative"***

*Baha'u'llah* died in May 29, 1892 from illness, appointing his son, Abbas Effendi—known by the title of *'Abdu'l-Baha* (Servant of *Baha*)—as his successor and the new leader of the *Baha'i* Faith.

## Succession

The appointment of *'Abdu'l-Baha* as "Head of the Faith" soon triggered an opposition from his family—particularly his half-brother, Mirza Muhammad 'Ali—who had been named second in rank to *'Abdu'l-Baha* by *Baha'u'llah.* Out of envy for his brother's position, Muhammad 'Ali began to plot a rebellion against him with the aid of his brothers,

Badi'u'llah and Diya'u'llah, in order to drive *'Abdu'l-Baha* out of power and establish himself as the sole leader of the faith. A majority of the *Baha'is* had unanimously accepted *'Abdu'l-Baha* as their righteous leader, having willingly embraced his leadership at the time, and were thus unmoved by the actions of Muhammad 'Ali, who was ultimately excommunicated from the *Baha'i* community for breaking the Covenant.

*'Abdu'l-Baha* then set out to deliver the message of his father across the world and spread the *Baha'i* Faith throughout Europe, North America and other continents. His strong leadership and unwavering efforts in preserving and promoting the teachings of the *Baha'i* Faith soon established him as one of the most prominent and influential *Baha'i* leaders in the West, being described in the early Western accounts of the *Baha'i* history in the following words:

*"The pilgrims brought back the sense of the early days of the faith, when the Prophet has been seen by human eyes and heard by human ears, and the world is filled with ecstasy like the golden light of perfect dawn."*

—The *Baha'i* Centenary

*Baha'i* communities began to establish across the United States and Canada, as *'Abdu'l-Baha* continued to visit several churches, missions and institutions to convey the *Baha'i* message of the unity of God and oneness of all humanity, welcoming people from all races and religions.

In his final years after World War I, he returned to the city of Haifa, where he was visited by a number of his devotees and pilgrims. Before his death on April 27, 1920, *'Abdu'l-Baha* composed his *Will and Testament* which laid down the structure of the *Baha'i* administrative order and set up institutions of the appointed Guardianship and authorized the Universal House of Justice as the supreme legislative institution to exercise judicial authority under the *Baha'i* Faith. It was also in his *Will and Testament* that he named his eldest grandson, Shoghi Effendi Rabbani, as his successor.

After the death of his grandfather, Effendi devoted much of his life to translating the sacred texts and scriptures of the *Baha'i* Faith and it was under his leadership that the *Baha'i* Faith expanded into a global religion, drawing scores of converts worldwide and multiplying *Baha'i* representation in several countries. During the 1940's, he began to work for the formation of the *Baha'i* World Center—the spiritual and administrative center of the *Baha'i* Faith—in Haifa, Israel, which involved the construction of the International Archives as well as the renovation of the shrines of the *Bab* and *Baha'u'llah.* The *Baha'i* World Center went on to become the central destination of pilgrimage for the *Baha'i* community today.

Effendi's sudden and unexpected death in the year 1957 ultimately left the *Baha'i* Faith without a chosen Guardian and the *Hands of the Cause* appointed by him as protectors of the faith thereby all unanimously concluded that their leader had died *"without having appointed his successor."*

Following the election of the Universal House of Justice in 1963, it was ruled on the basis of *'Abdu'l-Baha's* Will and Testament that no succeeding Guardian was possible to be appointed under the respective circumstances. The Universal House of Justice was thus established as the supreme governing body of the *Baha'i* Faith and remains to function as such to date, with its elections being held every five years.

4

## Beliefs and Teachings

The central message of the *Baha'i* teachings is essentially embedded in the doctrine of Love and Unity—epitomized by *Abdu'l-Baha* in his description of the term *"Baha'i"*:

> *"To be a Baha'i simply means to love all the world; to love humanity and try to serve it; to work for universal peace and universal brotherhood."*
>
> — ***Baha'u'llah and the New Era***

From this doctrine stem the basic fundamental beliefs of the *Baha'i* Faith that are embodied in a concept referred to as *"the three onenesses"*—the *Oneness of God,* the *Oneness of Humanity* and the *Oneness of Religion.*

## *The Oneness of God*

Being a monotheistic religion, the *Baha'i* Faith views God as a single omnipotent entity who is the source of all existence and the sustainer of all life, omnipresent and eternal, with no beginning or end. His power and Being are believed to be infinite and unknowable and exist beyond the capacity of the human mind to fully grasp or comprehend, described by *Baha'u'llah* as *"a unity which is exalted above all limitations, that transcendeth the comprehension of all created things."*

Due to its limitations, human language too is considered to fall short in completely and adequately expressing the Nature of the Divine. As such, the *Baha'i* Faith teaches that the only means to obtaining the knowledge of God is through the knowledge of His traits and attributes that are physically visible and perceptible to us. According to *Baha'u'llah,* these attributes are contained in all of God's creation and the best and most accurate reflection of His Being can thus be found in those who are the best and most refined of His creation—the Divine Messengers and *Manifestations of God.*

The *Baha'i* Faith teaches that by observing and reflecting the lives and teachings of God's Messengers we can learn more about the Nature of God, but to truly know God and be closer to Him, we must first learn to love Him. It is believed that in order to love God we must love and embrace His attributes and the attributes of His Messengers by incorporating them into our lives, such that they may reflect through us. The *Baha'i* teachings further illustrate that proximity to God can be obtained by selflessly devoting oneself to God and to all of humanity and by demonstrating love and kindness to all of His creation. Since love alone is the single most powerful force connecting us all with the universe and the Divine, the *Baha'i* belief holds that it is therefore solely in a state of love that we can become one with God and experience the Truth. *'Abdu'l-Baha* beautifully captures the essence of Love in the following excerpt from his writings:

*"Love is the light that guideth in darkness, the living link that uniteth God with man, that assureth the progress of every illumined soul. Love is the most great law that ruleth this mighty and heavenly cycle, the unique power that bindeth together the diverse elements of this material world, the supreme magnetic force that directeth the movements of the spheres in the celestial realms. Love revealeth with unfailing and*

*limitless power the mysteries latent in the universe. Love is the spirit of life unto the adorned body of mankind, the establisher of true civilization in this mortal world, and the shedder of imperishable glory upon every high-aiming race and nation."*

—Selections from the Writings of *'Abdu'l-Baha*

## *The Oneness of Humanity*

The *Baha'i* belief in the *Oneness of Humanity* is rooted in the teaching that the entire human race has been created in the *"image of God"* and is therefore regarded as equal in the eyes of God, transcending the boundaries and divisions of race, religion, ethnicity, gender and social distinction. The central idea underlying this belief states that since all of humanity is created equal, we all share the same basic capacities within, and all the differences that exist between us are therefore superficial and man-made. As such, every person in the world has a right to equal opportunities and fair treatment. According to the *Baha'i* teachings, humanity was inherently created as a single unit by God, but our ego, ignorance and selfish desires have blinded us from realizing this truth, as we continue to create divisions amongst ourselves and discriminate against one another. It is this prejudice that has given birth to the social, economic and political disparity that exists across the world and accounts for the prevalence of unequal opportunities between different sections of the world's population.

The intrinsic unity of all humanity is emphasized in the words of *Baha'u'llah,* who defined the entire human race as *"the fruit of one tree and the leaves of one branch." The Baha'i* teachings therefore highlight the pressing need for humanity to eradicate all forms of discrimination and prejudice that exists between us, stating that it is the only means to achieving world unity so we may all live together in harmony and peaceful coexistence. It is for this purpose that the *Baha'i* leaders always encouraged racial integration and approached members from diverse backgrounds while spreading their message and promoting their faith, so as to establish a sense of oneness amongst them, irrespective of their differences.

*While stressing upon the call for establishing unity and oneness between humanity, the Baha'i* teachings, at the same time, distinguish this unity from uniformity, by recognizing and upholding our individuality which makes us all unique in our own different way, as God created us. Instead of suppressing our diversity, the *Baha'i* Faith therefore teaches us to embrace it and celebrate it, while respecting the values and beliefs of others.

The beauty of this diversity is expressed by *'Abdu'l-Baha* in the following words:

*"The world of humanity is like unto a rose garden and the various races, tongues and people are like unto contrasting flowers. The diversity of colors in a rose-garden adds to the charm and beauty of the scene as variety enhances unity."*

—'Abdu'l-Baha, *Divine Philosophy*

It is thus in the acceptance and tolerance of this diversity, *Abdu'l-Baha* states, that we can truly recognize the beauty within ourselves and each other and collectively make our world a more beautiful place.

## *The Oneness of Religion*

The belief in the unity of Religion lies at the heart of the *Baha'i* teachings and holds that all the major spiritual leaders and founders of different religions who have come to the world have been sent by God as his *Manifestations* and Prophets to reveal a single religious Truth, under a single Divine plan for all of humanity, through a process known as "*progressive revelation*". The *Baha'i* teachings thus illustrate that despite their external differences, all religions inherently share the same foundations and reveal the same Divine Truth, as highlighted in the message of the Universal House of Justice:

> *"God is one and that, beyond all diversity of cultural expression and human interpretation, religion is likewise one."*

**— The Universal House of Justice, *Message to the World's Religious Leaders***

*Baha'u'llah* held that all of humanity is continually engaged in a process of collective evolution and growth, which he compared to the evolution of an individual. Initially born a helpless infant, the individual learns from his surroundings and gradually matures into an adult. Humanity, likewise, begins its physical and spiritual journey at a primitive stage and slowly continues to evolve until it reaches maturity. *Baha'u'llah* illustrated this collective evolution by highlighting how each Divine Messenger and *Manifestation of God* came with a greater revelation than the preceding one in order to meet the needs and conditions of the age of civilizations, as they continually evolved and matured over time. Thus, all *Manifestations of God* and founders of all major religions, including Zoroaster, Krishna, Moses, Buddha, Jesus and Muhammad, preached the same religious Truth through different laws and precepts by establishing different social systems, thereby aiding and nurturing humanity's process of collective evolution.

As such, all the *Manifestations of God* are believed to possess the same Divine attributes and similarly fulfill the same purpose by conveying the word of God to His creation, with neither one being superior to the other. Similarly, *Baha'u'llah* never claimed to be the last *Manifestation,* stating instead, that the process of revelation will continue into the future where humanity will witness the coming of many more *Manifestations. Baha'u'llah* has emphasized the recognition and acceptance of each one of these *Manifestations* as being equivalent to the acceptance of God Himself, stating:

*"God hath ordained the knowledge of these sanctified Beings to be identical with the knowledge of His own Self. Whoso recognizeth them hath recognized God. Whoso hearkeneth to their call, hath hearkened to the Voice of God, and whoso testifieth to the truth of their Revelation, hath testified to the truth of God Himself. Whoso turneth away from them, hath turned away from God, and whoso disbelieveth in them, hath disbelieved in God."*

**—Gleanings from the Writings of *Baha'u'llah***

## Principles of the *Baha'i* Faith

The writings of *Baha'u'llah* shed light upon the fundamental principles of the faith necessary for all of humanity to abide by. These principles were later built on by his son *'Abdu'l-Baha,* who introduced the *Baha'i* Faith to different parts of the world by addressing them as the essential guidelines imperative for the physical and spiritual growth and progress of the entire human race.

Some of the basic principles laid down by the *Baha'i* Faith include:

### *The independent investigation of Truth*

One of the most important principles underlying the *Baha'i* Faith is the independent investigation of the Divine Truth, which calls on every individual of the world to set out in pursuit of knowledge in order to free oneself from *"the weeds of ignorance, thorns of superstitions and thistles of imitations"* and obtain the ultimate *"Reality."*

The *Baha'i* Faith teaches that God has bestowed every human being with the equal capacity to use their own individual reasoning as a means of deriving their own independent conclusions and unveiling their own Truth. As such, every individual is obligated to independently seek this Truth on their own terms, as opposed to blindly following and accepting the word of any particular tradition, ideology or doctrine without question. The dangers of falling into the trap of ignorance by failing to go on an independent search for Truth are highlighted by *Baha'u'llah* in the following extract from his writings:

*"But as they failed to recognize the accents of God and the divine mysteries and holy allusions enshrined in that which flowed from the tongue of Muhammad, and as they neglected to examine the matter in their own hearts, and followed instead those priests of error who have hindered the progress of the people in past dispensations and who will continue to do so in future cycles, they were thus veiled from the divine purpose, failed to quaff from the celestial streams, and deprived themselves of the presence of God, the Manifestation of His Essence, and the Dayspring of His eternity."*

**—Baha'u'llah, *Gems of Divine Mysteries***

At the same time, it is considered equally important to begin this quest for Truth with a pure heart and sincere intentions in order to overcome all the obstacles along the way that lie *"between man and God." Baha'u'llah* has referred to these obstacles as the *"three barriers"* which include the *"attachment to the things of this world,"* the *"attachment to the rewards of the next world,"* and the *"attachment to the Kingdom of Names."* These barriers simply serve to veil God's presence from us and distract us from the Truth. He therefore instructed the seeker of knowledge to *"consume the egotistical veils with the fire of oneness"* and seek the Truth *"sincerely for the sake of God."*

Since God alone is the single Source of all knowledge, the *Baha'i* Faith teaches that all those who set out to acquire the Truth with honest intentions will ultimately be led to Him and thus unite on the basis of a common Truth.

## *The Unity of science and religion*

Humanity has remained divided for centuries in the conflict between science and religion, stemming from the contradictory nature and interpretation of scientific thought and traditional religious beliefs.

The *Baha'i* teachings reject the notion that true science stands in opposition of true religion, deeming it false and inaccurate and instead, call for the harmonization of science and religion. Since one of the central tenets of the *Baha'i* Faith is the belief in the oneness of Reality and Truth, the *Baha'i* teachings assert that religious truth therefore cannot exist independently of scientific truth.

*Baha'u'llah* has emphasized the importance of reason and rationality, referring to the human mind as a *"gift"* from God which enables us to *"discern the truth in all things" and "discover the secrets of creation."* The *Baha'i* teachings *thus state that only difference between the conclusions deduced by science and religion is that scientific truths are discovered by means of reason, whereas religious truths are divinely revealed. Since God alone is the Source of both reason and knowledge, who sends down His revelations to man and enables us to discover the truth with the mind that He blessed us with, science and religion both ultimately offer different aspects of the same Divine*

*Truth. Any contradictions that exist between the two are therefore believed to be the product of the human distortion of Truth over the course of time, which has corrupted the true message of God and resulted in the misrepresentation and misinterpretation of the original religious scriptures. Similarly, the deviation of science from God over the centuries has in turn, further contributed to increasing the gap between science and religion. The importance of scientific and religious unity is emphasized by 'Abdu'l-Baha,* who has stated that when science is pursued without the aid of religion, it leads to *"materialism,"* whereas religion that is devoid of science, alternatively leads to *"superstition."* He expressed the need to achieve this unity in the following words, which highlight the complimentary relationship between the two:

*"Religion and science are the two wings upon which man's intelligence can soar into the heights, with which the human soul can progress. It is not possible to fly with one wing alone!"*

—'Abdu'l-Baha, *Paris Talks*

## *Equality between men and women*

Equality of the sexes is one of basic and fundamental principles of the *Baha'i* Faith, which emphasizes the need to eliminate all forms of inequality and discrimination that exist between men and women who are both regarded *"equal in the sight of God."* As such, the *Baha'i* Faith has continually promoted the emancipation of women in the world and encouraged the advancement of their full rights and liberties as individuals, who possess the same capacity and potential for contributing to the progress of society as men. The achievement of gender equality is acknowledged by the faith as one of the most important *"prerequisites of peace,"* highlighted in the statement by the Universal House of Justice which asserts:

*"Only as women are welcomed into full partnership in all fields of human endeavor will the moral and psychological climate be created in which international peace can emerge."*

**— The Universal House of Justice, *The Promise of World Peace***

The *Baha'i* teachings stress upon the need maintain a balance between the feminine and masculine forces of society, stating that the feminine nature and influence which is associated with kindness, nurturing and empathy, is essential for the advancement and achievement of world peace. The importance of acquiring this balance is expressed by *'Abdu'l-Baha,* who has referred to men and women as the *"two wings"* of humanity, stating:

*"So long as these two wings are not equivalent in strength, the bird will not fly. Until womankind reaches the same degree as man, until she enjoys the same arena of activity, extraordinary attainment for humanity will not be realized; humanity cannot wing its way to heights of real attainment. When the two wings or parts become equivalent in strength, enjoying the same prerogatives, the flight of man will be exceedingly lofty and extraordinary."*

**— 'Abdu'l-Baha, *The Promulgation of Universal Peace***

The *Baha'i* teachings regard the lack of equal social and educational opportunities between men and women as being accountable for the marginalization of women around the world, stating that the advancement of women's education is imperative, not simply to increase female participation in various professional and academic fields, but also for the shaping and molding of future generations that are raised by them. The *Baha'i* community has thus made tremendous efforts to promote and advance the rights of women, who account for 30 percent of the elected leadership in *Baha'i* councils at a national level, compared to an average of just 10 percent in national parliaments worldwide.

## *Universal education*

The *Baha'i* teachings regard education as a key principle of the faith, deeming the acquisition of universal education and knowledge the compulsory right of all humanity, which enables them to evolve both physically and spiritually as a civilization. The *Baha'i* Faith teaches that the progress and prosperity of every nation is essentially dependent on education, as it is the educated and learned masses who lead their nations toward success and advancement.

*Baha'u'llah* stressed on the importance of acquiring an education, stating that it is a lack of education, knowledge and understanding that causes societies to fall into disarray and ignorance, depriving man of *"that which he doth inherently possess."* He thus regarded education as the tool which holds the key to unlocking the God-given potentials hidden within each individual and enables them to recognize their purpose in this world, writing:

> *"Regard man as a mine rich in gems of inestimable value. Education can, alone, cause it to reveal its treasures, and enable mankind to benefit therefrom."*

***—Tablets of Baha'u'llah***

The *Baha'i* teachings lay particular emphasis on the promotion of a moral and spiritual education and consider it equally essential for the intellectual growth and development of the individual as the sciences, arts and other disciplines. *'Abdu'l-Baha* expressed the importance of moral and spiritual teachings by stating that literacy which is devoid of moral and spiritual conduct becomes meaningless and defeats the entire purpose of education. He thus insisted that if children are *"trained to be both learned and good,"* they can work wonders and *"cast their beams like brilliant candles on the world."*

The *Baha'i* teachings state that it is the primary obligation and duty of parents to ensure that their children receive a proper education and emphasize that special consideration should be given to the education of women who are considered the *"first educators."*

## *A Universal Language*

The principle of a single universal language stems from the basic *Baha'i* belief in the *oneness of humanity,* which calls for the elimination of all barriers that divide mankind, so we may all come together and unite on common and equal grounds. The *Baha'i* teachings focus on the need to establish a powerful and effective means of communication between societies and nations in order to facilitate the exchange of knowledge, ideas and information between them and enable them to engage in peaceful dialogue with one another.

The existence of such a vast variety of different languages that are spoken across various cultures and societies, however, are believed to act as a hindrance to unity and peace, being the root of all misunderstandings and miscommunication that prevail between them. The *Baha'i* teachings therefore urge humanity to adopt a common secondary language, in addition to their own native tongue, which should be taught in schools and incorporated into their curriculums, in order to eliminate the communication gap that exists between different nations and cultures, so they may reach a mutual understanding with one another and establish a sense of unity. *'Abdu'l-Baha* has highlighted the importance of developing a universal international language by declaring it the solution to all the problems of the world, which possesses the power to transform humanity *"from many families into one"* and *"gather the nations under one standard, as if the five continents of the world had become one."*

At the same time, the *Baha'i* teachings maintain that this universal language should not, by any means, undermine the local languages of different cultures and nations, who are encouraged to preserve and uphold their own mother tongue as their primary language. The universal language, which serves as a secondary language, is thus understood to function outside of the mother tongue, solely for the purpose of inter-communication between different communities of the world in order to establish a sense of unity between them.

## *A Universal Commonwealth*

One of the central components underlying the *Baha'i* teachings—the belief in the oneness of humanity—postulates the unification of all nations of the world under a single universal commonwealth. *Baha'u'llah* referred to the Earth as *"one country,"* with the entire human race constituting *"its citizens,"* and envisioned the establishment of a world commonwealth, whereby all nations, races and classes would come together to eliminate all divisions and boundaries that separate them, and *"lay the foundations of the world's Great Peace."* This commonwealth would be marked by a universal legislature composed of members who would serve as the *"trustees"* of all humanity, managing the resources of nations, regulating the life of people and securing and satisfying all their needs in a just and equitable manner. An international court would be established to resolve all disagreements between nations, along with an international executive, which would be responsible for implementing the laws and decisions of the legislative bodies, whilst protecting and preserving the unity of the entire commonwealth.

It is under this commonwealth, that a universal auxiliary language would thus function as a means of intercommunication between nations, and science and religion would finally be reconciled, enabling humanity to achieve physical and spiritual progress and thrive collectively as a people.

This commonwealth would ensure the equal participation of all people—particularly those belonging to the grassroots—and provide a voice to all of humanity. At the same time, it would defend and uphold the autonomy of every nation and preserve the rights and liberties of the people, while protecting their cultural traditions.

The grandson of *'Abdu'l-Baha,* Shoghi Effendi, regarded the establishment of this commonwealth as the beginning of *"the age in which the face of the earth, from pole to pole, will mirror the ineffable splendors of the Abha Paradise,"* describing it in the following words:

*"A world federal system, ruling the whole earth and exercising unchallengeable authority over its unimaginably vast resources, blending and embodying the ideals of both the East and the West, liberated from the curse of war and its miseries, and bent on the exploitation of all the available sources of energy on the surface of the planet, a system in which Force is made the servant of Justice, whose life is sustained by its universal recognition of one God and by its allegiance to one common Revelation."*

**—Shoghi Effendi, *The World Order of***

## The Covenant of *Baha'u'llah*

The Covenant is a sacred pact, described by the Universal House of Justice as *"a binding agreement between God and man,"* which forms the basis of the *Baha'i* Faith. Established by *Baha'u'llah* as a means to safeguard and preserve the unity of all humanity, the Covenant revived the Divine promise between God and His creation and ensured its continuity, while protecting his followers from being misled into creating divisions between them and splitting the religion into sects. Complete and absolute loyalty to this Covenant is sworn by every member of the *Baha'i* community, who are thus obligated to abiding by the provisions it has ordained.

The concept of the Covenant is one which has existed for thousands of years, as God sent down numerous Prophets and *Manifestations* in the past to deliver His Covenant and make it known to His people by means of *progressive revelation*—a process that constitutes one of the central *Baha'i* teachings. The *Baha'i* Faith thus recognizes all the major religious leaders of the past, including Zoroaster, Krishna, Moses, Buddha, Jesus and Muhammad, as the

*Manifestations of God* who revealed the same Divine Truth. As such, the primary duty prescribed by the Covenant entitles all members of the *Baha'i* community to pledge their allegiance to *"Him Who is the Dayspring of His Revelation and the Fountain of His laws, Who representeth the Godhead in both the Kingdom of His Cause and the world of creation."* This forms the first part of the Covenant, known as the *"Greater Covenant,"* which represents the covenant between the people and all the Divine Messengers and *Manifestations of God* that include *Baha'u'llah,* who was the recent, but not last, of the line of prophets that God has sent on Earth.

The second part of the Covenant, known as the *"Lesser Covenant,"* refers to the covenant between the people and the appointed successor of the faith. The question of leadership and succession was addressed by *Baha'u'llah* in *Kitab-i-'Ahd* (The Book of the Covenant), where he laid down the guidelines and obligations regarding the Covenant and appointed his son, *'Abdu'l-Baha* as his successor, urging his followers to *"their faces towards the Most Mighty Branch"* and embrace his leadership.

The obligations of the Covenant that are outlined by *Baha'u'llah* do not merely entail the recognition and acceptance of the new *Manifestation*, but also call on people to follow and practice his teachings while adhering to them faithfully, stating that whoever turns away from him has, in essence, *"turned away from the Messengers of the past and showeth pride towards God from all eternity to all eternity."*

*'Abdu'l-Baha* has expressed the *"power"* and significance of this Covenant by referring to it as a *"Lifeboat"* which serves as *"an Ark of Salvation,"* stating:

*"All true followers of the Blessed Perfection are sheltered and protected in this Ark. Whoever leaves it, trusting in his own will and strength, will drown and be destroyed. For the Blessed Perfection left no possibility for discord, disagreement, and dissension."*

**—'Abdu'l-Baha, *Ten days in the Light of Akka***

## The *Baha'i* view of good and evil

The *Baha'i* Faith regards all humans as fundamentally spiritual beings who are born inherently good and "*noble*" as God's creation. As such, every innate physical instinct and faculty within us serves an important purpose that is necessary for the functioning of the human body and the development of the soul. *Baha'u'llah* has thus emphasized the need to achieve a balance between one's mind, body and soul, through the disciplined expression of these natural biological instincts. For instance, the human sexual drive is considered to be a gift from God which—upon finding expression within the sacred bond of marriage—translates into a powerful spiritual union between a man and a woman based on love. The same gift, however, if exploited and abused, may have the opposite effect, ultimately leading to destructive actions that harm not only the individual, but those around him. The *Baha'i* teachings therefore stress upon the principle of moderation and self-restraint, which states that everything is beneficial to the individual as long as it remains within the bounds of moderation, but once it exceeds those bounds, it inevitably becomes destructive.

The *Baha'i* belief highlights the importance of the

*"special faculty"* of free will that God has bestowed all human beings with, asserting that it is this free will which gives us the liberty to make our own conscious choices in the world and enables us to freely live our lives according to our own wishes. At the same time, our free will also renders us responsible for our own actions in life. It is thus the demonstration of our free will which ultimately determines our actions as *"good"* or *"evil."* *'Abdu'l-Baha* has distinguished between two kinds of choices that govern our existence: the first includes those choices that are *"subject to the free will of man, such as justice, equity, tyranny and injustice, in other words, good and evil actions."* The latter, on the other hand, includes those physical factors that lie beyond the control of the individual and comprises all actions *"to which man is forced and compelled, such as sleep, death, sickness, decline of power, injuries and misfortunes."* He thus stated that man is *"free"* when it comes to *"the choice of good and bad actions."*

As such, the *Baha'i* Faith rejects the doctrine of *"original sin"* and denies the existence of an external evil force which physically manifests in the devil or Satan. The *Baha'i* teachings recognize the recurring subject of Satan in earlier religious scriptures as figurative allusions to the inner devil that resides within human beings, as opposed to literal references to an evil physical entity that exists independently of us. Satan is thus regarded as a reflection of the human being's *"lower nature"* that is embedded in our *"ego." Baha'u'llah* has referred to the ego as the *"Evil One"* who *"hindereth the rise and obstructeth the spiritual progress of the children of men."* This *Evil One,* he warned, is constantly *"lying in wait, ready to entrap you,"* and urged his followers to protect themselves from falling prey to him, stating:

*"Gird yourselves against his wicked devices, and, led by the light of the name of the All-Seeing God, make your escape from the darkness that surroundeth you. Let your vision be world-embracing, rather than confined to your own self."*

**—Baha'u'llah, *Tablets of Baha'u'llah***

Evil is thus described in the *Baha'i* teachings as the *"absence of good,"* just as darkness is the absence of light. Similarly, sin is regarded as an inevitable part of our fallible human existence, which teaches us to strive for self-improvement and redeem ourselves through repentance by turning to God, the *"All-Merciful,"* who *"forgiveth even the most grievous of sins."* Since none of us are free from sin, the *Baha'i* Faith forbids all people from attacking one another for the sins we are all guilty of within, and instead calls on everyone to demonstrate kindness and compassion toward each other and try to help one another to correct our faults.

The *Baha'i* Faith teaches that whatever serves as an obstacle to one's spiritual growth and progress is negative, while that which contributes to spiritual progress is positive. Everyone is therefore encouraged to seek spiritual progress out of their own free will, rather than being driven to do so by external force. Adib Taherzadeh—a prominent *Baha'i* writer who served as a member of the Universal House of Justice—emphasized the importance of free will in terms of one's relationship with God, stating:

*"A meaningful covenant between God and man must require freedom of choice on both sides, and that man must exercise his free will in choosing his response to his Creator."*

**—Adib Taherzadeh, *The Covenant of Baha'u'llah***

## The belief in life after death

The *Baha'i* teachings recognize the existence of a soul which is ethereal, rational and enduring in nature and defines the inherent identity of every individual that God created. It is this soul which gives life to the human body and hence, just like the physical body, the soul also grows and evolves through the spiritual development of the individual, while remaining *"independent of all infirmities of body or mind."*

Similarly, just as an individual nurtures the physical body and satisfies its biological and material needs and demands, the soul too has an appetite that must be satisfied in order to cultivate one's spirituality and allow the soul to progress and mature. The basic "food" for the soul is thus believed to be the innate goodness of a human being which stems from the demonstration of love, compassion, faith, courage, selflessness and humility—attributes which essentially reflect the virtues of God. Demonstrating love, kindness and compassion would thus not only enable an individual to achieve spiritual growth, but would also serve to bring them closer to God.

Since the soul, unlike the physical body, is created immortal, it continues to live on after the body dies, being thus liberated from the physical world and entering the next life in the spiritual world. *Baha'u'llah* has compared the process of life and death to rebirth, stating that the next world is "as *different from this world as this world is different from that of the child while still in the womb of its mother.*"

The parallel of an individual's life in the physical world to that of an unborn child that exists inside the womb of the mother, serves to highlight the significance of this world in terms of the next. Just as the womb provides a home for the human being's initial stage of physical development, this world constitutes a temporary place for the spiritual development and preparation of the soul for the "*world beyond.*"

The *Baha'i* teachings therefore urge every individual to detach oneself from worldly temptations and desires and live life in submission to the Will of the Creator so as to reflect His attributes alone, in order for the soul to acquire Paradise—a station "*so exalted,*" whose "*loftiness and glory…no tongue can adequately reveal, nor any other earthly agency describe.*"

It is thus one's personal relationship with God that is developed and nurtured by following the path of his *Manifestations,* which allows them to cleanse and purify their souls and ascend to "*the throne of the Most High*" after death. Those who "*live in error*" and turn away from God and His Messengers, however, are warned of their fate in the next life, where they would suffer and *"bemoan their plight."*

As such, Heaven and Hell are believed to symbolically represent spiritual states or conditions associated with one's proximity to or separation from God, as opposed to literal places.

At the same time, *Baha'u'llah* has continued to emphasize the hidden mysteries of the afterlife that remain concealed from all humanity, claiming that all his words and descriptions fail to adequately portray its true nature which can ultimately *"never be described, nor is it meet and permissible to reveal its whole character to the eyes of men."*

# 5

## Sacred writings and scriptures

The religious texts and scriptures of the *Baha'i* Faith are composed of the writings of the founders and successors of the faith, which include the *Bab, Baha'u'llah, 'Abdu'l-Baha* and Shoghi Effendi. At the same time, there is believed to be a distinction between these writings in terms of Divine revelation and the authoritative interpretation and instruction of the teachings.

Being the spiritual precursor of *Baha'u'llah,* the *Bab* is regarded as a central figure of the *Baha'i* Faith and acknowledged by the *Baha'i* community as a founder of the religion, alongside *Baha'u'llah.* As such, his writings, along with those of *Baha'u'llah,* are considered to be Divine revelations, being thus referred to as *"revealed texts."* The writings of the latter, which include the works of *'Abdu'l-Baha* and Shoghi Effendi, on the other hand, are not regarded as divinely revealed *Baha'i* scripture, but are rather considered to be authoritative interpretations of these texts and their teachings. Being appointed by *Baha'u'llah* as his successor to the faith, *'Abdu'l-Baha* was thus authorized by him as the only authentic interpreter of the *revealed texts,* just as Shoghi Effendi was appointed by *'Abdu'l-Baha* to succeed him after his death.

As such, the most important and sacred *Baha'i* scripture therefore constitutes the *revealed texts* of the *Bab* and *Baha'u'llah.*

The writings of the *Bab* include a variety of texts comprising hundreds of volumes and letters that often termed his *tablets,* much of which were lost in the midst of the intense persecution he was subjected during his time, along with his followers. As a result, only a small fraction of his authentic works remain available today which were written largely in Persian and Arabic. Of these writings, the most prominent and well-known text is considered to be that of the *Qayyum ul-Asma* (The Enduring of Names)—his earliest work, produced in the year 1844, and popularly dubbed *"the Quran of the Babis."* Other major works by him include the *Bayan*—a comprehensive treatise on social teachings, law and eschatology—which contained his prophecy about the messianic figure of *"He whom God shall make manifest,"* and the *Seven Proofs,* which laid down the proofs of his mission.

Despite much of his social laws and provisions later being superseded by those of *Baha'u'llah,* his work still remains significant in the *Baha'i* community today, with *Baha'u'llah* himself implementing some of it, such as the *Baha'i* calendar originally introduced by him.

The most prominent and important *Baha'i* scripture consists of the divinely inspired writings of *Baha'u'llah*—most notably, the *Kitab-i-Aqdas* (the Most Holy Book)—the central religious book of the *Baha'i* Faith, which shares the same status as the Bible for Christians and the Quran for Muslims. The *Kitab-i-Aqdas was composed in Arabic and completed by Baha'u'llah* in the year 1873, becoming established as the *"Mother Book"* of the *Baha'i* Faith. *Commonly referred to as the Book of Laws, the Aqdas laid down the religious, social and theological teachings of the faith and established its administrative institutions, laws and practices.*

Other major works of *Baha'u'llah* include the *Kitab-i-Iqan* (the Book of Certitude), which comprised spiritual and moral teachings for humanity and formed the basis of the *Baha'i* beliefs; the *Hidden Words,* a collection of short sayings and utterances containing spiritual truths; the two mystical treatises known as the *Seven Valleys* and the *Four Valleys;* and *Kitab-i-'Ahd* (Book of the Covenant)—*Baha'u'llah's* Will and Testament—where he named his son, *'Abdu'l-Baha,* as his successor.

*'Abdu'l-Baha* is believed to have written an estimate of over 27,000 tablets during his lifetime, out

of which, only a small proportion has been translated into English. His major works include *The Secret of Divine Civilization,* an extensive treatise on social and economic development that is regarded by the *Baha'i* community as a central authoritative book of the faith; and *A Traveller's Narrative*—a book illustrating the history of the *Bab* and the *Baha'i* Faith. A large collection of his public lectures and speeches have also been translated in English—most notably, the series of talks titled *"Some Answered Questions" dealing with religious and spiritual themes and questions regarding God, prophet-hood, evolution, fate and reincarnation.*

*His grandson,* Shoghi Effendi, later translated a number of texts and writings by the *Bab, Baha'u'llah* and *'Abdu'l-Baha* into English, such as the *Kitab-Iqan, Gleanings* and *Epistle to the Son of the Wolf,* presenting authoritative guidelines for all future translations of the *Baha'i* scripture and writings.

Most of Effendi's writings consist of a vast collection of letters, amounting to a total estimate of 30,000, which deal with various religious, political and social themes. The most well-known of these letters include the *World Order of Baha'u'llah,* a series of messages regarding the *Baha'i* administration and institutions, and *Advent of Divine Justice,* which he addressed to the *Baha'is* of America and Canada, highlighting their role in the establishment of world peace. In 1944, he published his first and only full-length book titled *God Passes By,* the central text detailing various significant events of the *Baha'i* history, which also presented Effendi's own interpretation of the events.

In addition to these writings, the works produced by the Universal House of Justice also constitute an important part of the canonical texts of the *Baha'i* Faith. While the Universal House of Justice does not hold the power or authority to interpret the writings of the central figures and successors of the faith, it is authorized to address other issues or questions that have not been dealt with in those writings and scriptures. As such, its works are regarded as authoritative guidelines for the *Baha'i* community. Moreover, it is the primary function of the Universal House of Justice along with the International *Baha'i* Library to ensure the collection, authentication, translation and preservation of the *Baha'i* texts and scriptures.

6

## Religious customs and practices

According to the *Baha'i* teachings, the central purpose of human life is to know and love God. Prayer and meditation thus form an essential part of the spiritual growth and development of the individual, being referred to as the *"core of religious faith"* by *Baha'u'llah,* which enable one to experience a *"state of spiritual communion" with God. A tremendous amount of emphasis is laid on the "spiritual nourishment" of the individual, as Baha'u'llah* urged his followers to engage in meditation so that *"the secret of things unseen may be revealed unto you, that you may inhale the sweetness of a spiritual and imperishable fragrance."*

*Baha'u'llah* wrote numerous prayers designed for daily recitation, for the purpose of both spiritual and worldly success and development. The *Baha'i* teachings essentially distinguish between two forms of prayers—obligatory prayers and devotional prayers. Both forms of prayers are composed of words of praise and reverence for God and have different functions and instructions regarding their offering.

Obligatory prayers have been prescribed to all *Baha'is* between the age of 15 and 70, who are required to offer one of the three obligatory prayers—the *short,* the *medium* and the *long*—on a daily basis for the purpose of their personal spiritual growth. A specific time of the day has been prescribed for the offering of these prayers, which must be preceded by *ablution*—the ritual cleansing of the hands and face—and be offered facing the *Qiblih,* which marks the direction of the Shrine of *Baha'u'llah.*

Devotional prayers, on the other hand, are largely recited and offered for the purpose of personal success and gains, such as marriage, protection, etc. These prayers may be recited aloud or even sung, however, the original text should remain the same. As such, most of the conditions prescribed for obligatory prayers do not necessarily apply to general devotional prayers.

In addition to prayer and meditation, fasting also constitutes one of the central pillars of the *Baha'i* Faith, whereby all followers are instructed to observe fasts during a nineteen-day period every year. This period occurs during the *Baha'i* month of *'Ala* (between March 2 and March 20). Each fast that is observed during this month lasts from sunrise to sunset and involves the complete abstention from all forms of food and drink. Fasting is prescribed to all *Baha'is* once they reach the age of 15 and is considered obligatory, with certain exemptions depending on particular conditions and circumstances, for instance, illness or pregnancy.

The practice of fasting is regarded by the *Baha'i* teachings as an essential means of disciplining the body and soul and thus signifies a period of meditation, prayer and spiritual reflection, where the individual abstains not merely from food and drink, but from all forms of selfish desires and impulses stemming from the ego. *'Abdu'l-Baha* has described the practice of fasting as a means of *"awakening man" which causes one's heart to become "tender" and illuminates the soul "with the fire of divine love."*

*Baha'u'llah* has emphasized the importance of prayer and fasting in the following words:

*"Cling firmly to obligatory prayer and fasting. Verily, the religion of God is like unto heaven; fasting is its sun, and obligatory prayer is its moon. In truth, they are the pillars of religion whereby the righteous are distinguished from those who transgress His commandments."*

***—Selection of Extracts and Prayers from the Baha'i Writings***

## *The Baha'i House of Worship*

The *Baha'i* House of Worship marks the official place of worship for the *Baha'i* community, where followers of the faith gather to engage in prayer and meditation. Established by *Baha'u'llah* as the *"Dawning-place of the Remembrance of God,"* the *Baha'i* House of Worship serves as a center of the *Baha'i* spiritual life, where members from all backgrounds come together under its *"universal shelter."*

The House of Worship shares a similar status to that of a mosque, church or temple, but at the same time, was also envisioned by the leaders of the faith as a religious community center, surrounded by a complex of social, educational, humanitarian, scientific and medical institutions, all collectively functioning to remove *"the ills that have so long and so grievously afflicted humanity."*

The *Baha'i* teachings encourage the building of a House of Worship in every town and city, and emphasize its universality as a place of worship, that is designed to welcome people from all faiths and religious backgrounds to unite under a single roof for the purpose of worship—irrespective of their differences. As such, the sacred scriptures of all religions along with those of the *Baha'i* Faith are permitted to be read and recited in their respective languages. At the same time, the display of sculptures and images and the playing of musical instruments is prohibited inside the House of Worship, as is the delivery of sermons and organizing of ceremonies.

All Houses of Worship adhere to a set of common architectural requirements that serve as a symbol of unity and oneness—most notably their nine-sided circular shape. Furthermore, all the Houses of Worship that have been constructed to date have a single room built under the dome, with all seats facing the *Qiblih.*

At present, there are seven Houses of Worship that have been constructed worldwide, located in four different continents of the globe. These Houses of Worship are managed and administered by the National Spiritual Assembly representing the *Baha'i* community in the respective country where they are located.

The first House of Worship was constructed in Russia, in the city of Ashkhabad—the current capital of Turkmenistan—and completed in the year 1908. Being built under the supervision and protection of the Soviet Government, the Ashkhabad House of Worship soon became established as the spiritual and social center of the *Baha'i* community, drawing new converts whose numbers rapidly began to rise. The House of Worship was eventually expanded to build schools, medical institutions and a hostel for travelers and served the community for two decades, after being damaged in an earthquake and ultimately being demolished in 1962.

The next House of Worship was constructed in the United States, in the city of Wilmette, Illinois, in the year 1953. Merging the architectural designs and styles of both the East and the West, it soon became a popular Chicago-area landmark, attracting millions of visitors and tourists over the years. The Wilmette House of Worship remains to be the largest and oldest remaining House of Worship, referred to as the *"Mother temple of the West"* by the *Baha'i* community.

Following this, six other *Baha'i* Houses of Worship were subsequently constructed in various locations across the world, including Kampala, Uganda; Sydney, Australia; Frankfurt, Germany; Panama City, Panama; Tiapapata, Samoa; and Delhi, India.

About 123 sites across the world have been selected by the Universal House of Justice to build future Houses of Worship—with the construction of one currently underway in Santiago, Chile.

7

# *The Baha'i Symbol*

The *Baha'i* Faith is represented by the nine-pointed star, which serves as the official symbol of the religion. The Arabic term, "*Baha*" is believed to have a numerical value equivalent to that of the number 9. Moreover, the number 9 is also considered to possess great significance in numerology, as highlighted by Shoghi Effendi, who referred to it as "*the sign of perfection.*" The number 9 has been mentioned numerous times in the *Baha'i* history and teachings, for instance, it was nine years after the declaration of the *Bab*, that *Baha'u'llah* received his revelation from God, while imprisoned in Tehran. Being the highest single-digit number, it is also associated with completeness and is thus believed to reflect the "*fulfillment of expectations of all prior religions*" by the *Baha'i* Faith. Hence, all *Baha'i* Houses of Worship are constructed with 9 sides.

## Symbols of *Baha'i* Faith

# 8

## *Marriage and family life*

The family unit is viewed by the *Baha'i* teachings as a basic institution of society, where the home is regarded as a place filled with love, happiness and peace, tied together with the unity and brotherhood of all its members. *'Abdu'l-Baha* has described the home as the *"center for the diffusion of the light of divine guidance,"* which enables the *"dissemination of the Words of God"* and kindles *"the fire of love in the hearts of His faithful servants and maidservants."*

As such, the *Baha'i* teachings lay great emphasis upon the raising of the family in accordance with the *"rules of sanctity"* whereby the rights, roles and obligations of every member, including the spouse, the parents, the children and the siblings, must be equally realized with respect to one another. *'Abdu'l-Baha* has highlighted the importance of preserving and maintaining this unity through adherence to these rules, stating:

*"The injury of one shall be considered the injury of all; the comfort of each, the comfort of all; the honor of one, the honor of all."*

—'Abdu'l-Baha, *Promulgation of Universal Peace*

Marriage is considered to be the foundation of family life and regarded as the *"fortress for well-being and salvation."* It is described by the *Baha'i* teachings as the monogamous union between a man and a woman, whose bond surpasses the physical world and exits on a spiritual plane between the husband and wife. The marital bond is thus believed to have a divine status which defines marriage as a sacred institution, whose central purpose is to elevate the human race to *"the true station destined for it by God."* Though the *Baha'i* teachings do not regard marriage as an obligation, it is still seen as the *"moral duty"* of every individual, with the exception of a minority who, due to certain mental or physical *"deficiency,"* are incapacitated to enter into marriage. The pursuit of marital life is therefore highly encouraged as a natural and *"rightful"* way of life that is conducive to the social and spiritual growth and development of all humanity.

*'Abdu'l-Baha* has compared the life of a married couple to that of *"angels in heaven,"* whose thoughts must resemble *"the rays of the sun of truth and the radiance of the brilliant stars in the heavens."* The

husband and wife are thus urged to honor their bond and "*covenant*" and live in love and harmony with one another in order to experience "*perfect contentment*" and achieve "*divine grace and favor in the Kingdom of heaven.*"

The *Baha'i* teachings give all followers the complete freedom and liberty to choose their own marital partner without any form of pressure or interference from their parents and family members. At the same time, the consent and approval of one's living parents is considered equally important once the partner has been chosen, before proceeding with the marriage. The purpose of this law is to honor the relationship between the parent and child and strengthen the unity between both families.

The marriage ceremony is held differently according to the individual culture and traditions of the couple, while complying with certain basic religious obligations. The marriage must be conducted in the presence of two witnesses who are chosen by the *Baha'i* governing council, and involves the recitation of the following vows by both the bride and groom, as prescribed by *Baha'u'llah*:

"*We will all, verily, abide by the Will of God.*"

—*The Kitab-i-Aqdas*

The rest of the ceremony essentially includes the reading of the *Baha'i* scriptures and prayers, followed by music, dance, food and other festivities.

The *Baha'i* Faith defines marriage as the exclusive union between a man and a woman and all forms of sexual relations that are maintained outside of the marital bond are thus prohibited and discouraged—including homosexuality. Inter-marriage between members of different religions, races and ethnicities, however, is highly encouraged by the *Baha'i* teachings, which emphasize the oneness of humanity.

Equality between the husband and wife is considered essential within the marriage, in order to maintain a balance between their roles and duties and avoid conflict. As such, the wife has the freedom to work and pursue an independent career of her choice, while the husband is required to share the domestic duties with his wife.

9

# *The Baha'i Calendar*

The *Baha'i* calendar takes its roots from the *Bab'i* calendar—formally known as the *Badi'* Calendar (New Calendar)—which was originally introduced by the *Bab* in his writings. The calendar is built on the basis of a solar year and comprises 19 months, with each month consisting of 19 days, adding up to a total of 361 days, in addition to the intercalation period.

The calendar was later adopted by *Baha'u'llah* as the standard official calendar of the *Baha'i* Faith and the month of *Naw-Ruz* was declared the first day of the year to mark the commencement of the *Baha'i* era. The *Baha'i* calendar was also set to match the Gregorian calendar, so as to avoid variations between the two.

Each of the nineteen months has a different name which was originally ascribed by the *Bab*, and denotes the different attributes of God. Similarly, each day of the *Baha'i* week has also been given a different name, which starts from *Jalal* (Saturday) and ends on *Istiqlal* (Friday). Certain dates of the *Baha'i* calendar are regarded as sacred and include a total of eleven holy days, out of which, nine have been deemed religious holidays.

The festival of *Rivdan*—a twelve day period honoring *Baha'u'llah's* declaration and claim to prophet-hood—is considered the most sacred period and is popularly referred to as the *"Most Great Festival"* by the *Baha'i* community. The festival begins during the month of *Jalal* and the first, ninth and twelfth days of *Rivdan* constitute important *Baha'i* holidays whereby all work is suspended. The festival is essentially celebrated in community gatherings where people collectively engage in prayer on the three holidays. The *Baha'i* elections usually take place during *Rivdan*—a custom initiated during the time of *'Abdu'l-Baha*—where local spiritual assemblies are elected along with the Universal House of Justice.

In addition, the births of the *Bab* and *Baha'u'llah* are also celebrated along with the days of their declaration, *Baha'u'llah's* ascension and the martyrdom of the *Bab.*

## 10

## *The Baha'i pilgrimage*

The *Baha'i* pilgrimage—formally referred to as the *Suriy-i-Hajj*—has been prescribed as an obligatory duty that must be performed by all members of the *Baha'i* community who are physically and financially capable of performing it and *"no obstacle stands in one's way."*

The pilgrimage, which spans nine days, involves guided visits to the sacred shrines and sites of the *Baha'i* Holy Land, located at the *Baha'i* World Center in Israel. The three central sites of the pilgrimage include Bahji, Akka (Acre) and Haifa, each of whom has a historical and spiritual significance of its own.

The *Baha'i* Faith regards pilgrimage to the home of the *Manifestation* of God as being equivalent to visiting the home of God Himself. *'Abdu'l-Baha* emphasized the significance and sacredness of these holy sites and shrines, stating:

*"Holy places are undoubtedly centers of the outpouring of Divine grace, because on entering the illumined sites associated with martyrs and holy souls, and by observing reverence, both physical and spiritual, one's heart is moved with great tenderness."*

—'Abdu'l-Baha, *Synopsis and Codification of the Kitab-i-Aqdas*

Moreover, the coming together of *Baha'is* from various parts of the world, all belonging to different backgrounds and walks of life, helps to strengthen their unity and foster love and harmony between them.

Every year, the *Baha'i* World Center draws a massive influx of *Baha'i* pilgrims from around the world, who come to pay their respects to the Central Figures of the faith. The visit to the shrines of the *Bab, Baha'u'llah* and *'Abdu'l-Baha* thus serves as the fundamental obligation of all pilgrims, who gather to pray and meditate at *"the heart of the Qiblih."*

The Shrine of *Baha'u'llah* in Bahji is regarded as the most holy place for the *Baha'i* community and represents the official *Qiblih* of the faith which all *Baha'is* face during prayer. The remains of *Baha'u'llah* have been inferred in northwest corner of the complex near the Mansion of Bahji, which marks the first place visited by the *Baha'i* pilgrims. The visit to the shrine is also accompanied by a visit to his mansion and the

*Haram-i-Aqdas*—the "Holy Court" consisting of the gardens and the outer sanctuary of the shrine.

The shrines of the *Bab* and *'Abdu'l-Baha* at Haifa constitute the two most sacred *Baha'i* monuments after the shrine of *Baha'u'llah*, and are thus visited by the pilgrims next. Though the *Bab* was executed in Iran in 1850, *Baha'u'llah* later had his remains transferred to Mount Carmel in Israel, where his shrine was constructed by *'Abdu'l-Baha* in 1909. The remains of *'Abdu'l-Baha* have been temporarily laid to rest in one of the rooms inside the Shrine of the *Bab*, as a new structure is being planned for its relocation.

Other sites visited by pilgrims at Haifa include the Monument Gardens—a set of gardens consisting of the mausoleums of some members of *Baha'u'llah's* family—the Arc buildings of the *Baha'i* administration and the House of *'Abdu'l-Baha*.

The major sites visited by pilgrims at Akka consist mainly of the barracks where *Baha'u'llah* was imprisoned along with his companion in 1868, and the three houses where *Baha'u'llah* spent his last few months.

In addition to prayer and meditation, these visits predominantly comprise the recitation of the *Tablet of Visitation*—a tablet consisting of verses and passages from the writings of *Baha'u'llah*.

Apart from the sites of the Holy Land, the two most important designated places for the *Baha'i* pilgrimage include the House of the *Bab* in Shiraz, Iran, and the former residence of *Baha'u'llah* in Baghdad, known as the *"Most Great House,"* where he lived during his exile. These sites, along with a majority of others located in Iran and Iraq, however, are not accessible to a majority of the *Baha'is* due to the deep-rooted religious hostilities prevailing in the region that has long subjected the *Baha'i* community to persecution, particularly at the hands of the Shiite religious clergy, who have deemed the *Baha'i* Faith *"apostasy from Islam."* The House of the *Bab* has been destroyed twice in the midst of the religious unrest, while the House of *Baha'u'llah* was destroyed in June, 2013 in unknown circumstances.

Those who wish to perform pilgrimage may apply for it through the department of the *Baha'i* World Center, which is responsible for making special arrangements for the pilgrim's stay and transportation at Israel and provides them with the necessary guidance and information through their journey.

Despite being unable to visit the designated sites for pilgrimage in Iraq and Iran at present, the *Baha'is* remain hopeful for the future and look forward to being welcomed there one day.

## 11

## The *Baha'i* global community

Despite being the youngest of all independent world religions, the *Baha'i* Faith has successfully established itself as one of the world's fastest growing religions today, with approximately 7 million followers around the world, all belonging to diverse ethnic, racial and religious backgrounds and residing in more than 230 countries.

According to the *Baha'i* World Center, the *Baha'i* community has expanded to virtually every corner of the globe and currently constitutes the second most wide-spread religion after Christianity, in terms of the countries and nationalities it represents. The *Baha'i* community is composed of an estimated 2100 ethnic, racial and tribal groups who inhabit over 100,000 localities in different regions of the world, with a majority of the community residing in Asia, Africa and Latin America.

All communities have organized themselves in their respective countries through elected local councils known as National Spiritual Assemblies that govern the affairs of the community and religion. Israel serves as the international headquarters of the faith, where the center of the *Baha'i* Covenant—the Universal House of Justice—is seated in the city of Haifa.

Despite the vast diversity within various members of the *Baha'i* community, the most distinguished characteristic which defines them is the strong sense of oneness and unity that binds them together, through their commitment to a universal global ideology and system of beliefs and ideals centered on the social, spiritual and intellectual progress of all humanity and the achievement of world peace.

As such, *Baha'is* around the world have made efforts to maintain powerful networks of communication between one another, both within and across borders, in order to stay connected and collectively work for the promotion and preservation of their religion and its teachings. Several *Baha'i* communities around the world conduct local seminars and engage in meetings and discussions to address various humanitarian issues, such as gender inequality and racial discrimination, in order to eliminate all barriers of prejudice from society and establish a world where all of humanity lives in peaceful coexistence with one another.

Another unique feature of the *Baha'i* Faith is the absence of a religious clergy, which separates it from most major religions. As such, there are no sermons or liturgy and all members of the *Baha'i* community are encouraged to read scriptures of the faith independently, which have the final binding authority, and apply their teachings out of their own understanding. Being fairly modern, much of the *Baha'i* scriptures were personally composed by the founders of the faith in the 19th and 20th centuries and thus present firsthand accounts of its history and development that are relatively more accessible to modern generations of this age than the scriptures of most major religions which date back thousands of years.

Members of the *Baha'i* community conduct regular meetings and sessions to read and discuss their scriptures, which generally take place in the *Baha'i* centers or within their private homes. In addition, *Baha'is* are also committed to a variety of social and economic development programs that function in different parts of the world and cater to the needs of local communities. Most of these programs range from the provision of healthcare, educational, religious and social services, along with the establishment of environmental centers, orphanages and agricultural projects. Service to others is regarded as a form of worship in the *Baha'i* Faith, which benefits not only the worker, but society as a whole. As such, a number of *Baha'is* volunteer their time and resources to engage in social and economic development programs focused on promoting peace and welfare for all humanity.

In 1943, the first international non-governmental organization representing members of the *Baha'i* Faith was founded, titled the *Baha'i* International Community (BIC). Currently affiliated with more than 180 countries across the world, the central purpose and function as stated by the BIC is to promote the teachings of the *Baha'i* Faith and contribute to the establishment of a *"united, peaceful, just, and sustainable civilization."* In addition, it is also dedicated to the protection and advancement of human rights, gender equality, and the *"promotion of just and equitable means of global prosperity."*

The BIC works in collaboration with the United Nations and other non-governmental organizations around the world, with a number of offices operating in various locations, including New York, Rome, Brussels, Vienna and Geneva. Over the years, the BIC has achieved consultative status with the UN Economic and Social Council (ECOSOC) and the UN Children's Fund (UNICEF), in addition to pursuing joint initiatives and programs with several other United Nations agencies including the World Health Organization (WHO), the UN Environment Program (UNEP), the UN Development Fund for Women (UNIFEM) and the UN Children's Fund (UNICEF).

A central feature of the *Baha'i* community life is the Nineteen-Day Feast—a community gathering which takes place on the first day of every month of the *Baha'i* calendar. Open to all members of the *Baha'i* community, the Feast constitutes an administrative meeting merged with spiritual and devotional services aimed at strengthening the unity and bond between members and fostering their social and spiritual growth. As such, the Feast provides members of the community with the opportunity to communicate important issues and recommendations to the Local Spiritual Assemblies, in addition to engaging in devotional prayers and socialization. Though attendance at the Feast is not obligatory upon the *Baha'i* community, it is regarded as an important spiritual duty which has been described by *Baha'u'llah* as a means *"to bind your hearts together."*

The Feast typically consists of three programs, starting from devotional prayers, to administrative discussions that are followed by a period of socializing which is accompanied with drinks and refreshments for everyone.

The significance of the Nineteen-Day Feast has been highlighted by *'Abdu'l-Baha,* who referred to it as *"The Lord's Supper,"* comparing it to the Last Supper in Christianity:

*"Make ye an effort in every meeting that the Lord's Supper may become realized and the heavenly food descend. This heavenly food is knowledge, understanding, faith, assurance, love, affinity, kindness, purity of purpose, attraction of hearts and the union of souls ... When the meeting is conducted after this manner, then 'Abdu'l-Baha also is present in heart and soul, though His body may not be with you."*

— 'Abdu'l-Baha, *Baha'i World Faith*

## 12

## The Universal House of Justice

The Universal House of Justice serves as the center of the *Baha'i* administrative order, having the supreme international legislative authority of the administration. Officially founded in the year 1963, the Universal House of Justice was established as the supreme governing institution of the faith, whose structure, roles and functions had been laid down in the writings of *Baha'u'llah* and *'Abdu'l-Baha.* The institution is composed of nine members that are elected every five years by the national governing institutions of the *Baha'i* world, to serve as *"the Trustees of God amongst His servants and the daysprings of authority in His countries."*

As such, the basic functions of the Universal House of Justice are centered on governing the administrative, social and religious affairs of the global *Baha'i* community, which essentially include the promulgation of the laws and teachings of the *Baha'i* Faith and the expansion and development of its spiritual and administrative institutions; the administration and organization the affairs of the *Baha'i* community; and the advancement of *"universal peace"* through *"the realization of greater cordiality and comity amongst the nations."*

In addition, the Universal House of Justice is also responsible for *"the arbitration and settlement of disputes arising between people"* and the implementation of laws and sanctions for the establishment and protection of *"Divine Justice."* At the same, however, it does not possess the authority to alter any of the laws that have originally been prescribed in the *Baha'i* scriptures.

Since its inception, the Universal House of Justice has played an important role in providing guidance and support to members of the *Baha'i* community worldwide in the form of published letters and compilations addressing various themes of the *Baha'i* teachings. The institution has also been committed to the preservation of the sacred *Baha'i* writings and scriptures, having published numerous translations of the works of the *Bab, Baha'u'llah* and *'Abdu'l-Baha.* The research departments and archives established by Universal House of Justice at the *Baha'i* World Center have, over the years, managed to collect thousands of letters composed by the founders of the faith, which often serve as the basis of their public statements.

Keeping in line with the functions prescribed to the institution by *Baha'u'llah,* the Universal House of Justice has also undertaken a series of initiatives to address various global issues concerning human rights, social and economic development and the environment.

13

# *Baha'u'llah* and the prophetic fulfillment of world religions

*Baha'u'llah* is recognized by the *Baha'i* community as the embodiment of the universal *Promised One* of all world religions, whose coming marked the fulfillment of all messianic prophesies *"heralded in all the sacred Scriptures."* Highlighting the universality of his all-embracing message, *Baha'u'llah* addressed his proclamation to all religious communities of the world, calling out to *"the people of the Torah," "the people of the Evangel," "the people of the Quran"* and *"the Magians."* As such, *Baha'u'llah's* prophetic fulfillment of the *Babi* messenger, *"He Whom God Shall Manifest,"* is believed to reflect the amalgamation of six distinctive messianic figures from different religious traditions which include Judaism, Christianity, Islam, Zoroastrianism, Hinduism and Buddhism.

In his book titled *"God Passes By,"* *'Abdu'l-Baha's* grandson, Shoghi Effendi has described the *"multiple messiahship"* of *Baha'u'llah* as a reconciliation of the *"seemingly divergent claims and doctrines"* of these religions which led to *"the gradual unfoldment of one Divine Revelation,"* stating:

*"To Israel He was neither more nor less than the incarnation of the 'Everlasting Father,' the 'Lord of Hosts' come down 'with ten thousands of saints'; to Christendom Christ returned 'in the glory of the Father,' to Shi'ah Islam the return of the Imam Husayn; to Sunni Islam the descent of the 'Spirit of God' (Jesus Christ); to the Zoroastrians the promised Shah-Bahram; to the Hindus the reincarnation of Krishna; to the Buddhists the fifth Buddha."*

**—Shoghi Effendi, *God Passes By***

At the same time, while declaring himself the prophesied messiah of all religions, *Baha'u'llah* maintained that his claims served as a symbolic fulfillment of the messianic prophesies of these religions, as opposed to the literal. Each of the major world religions, for instance, emerged through the teachings of a single messianic figure who served as the spiritual guide of all future civilizations that followed him. As such, Moses is acknowledged as the central figure of Judaism and holds the same status as that of Jesus in Christianity, Krishna, in Hinduism and Muhammad, in Islam. According to the *Baha'i* concept of *progressive revelation,* each of these messengers and religious founders is believed to have been sent down by the same Divine Source to reveal the same Divine Truth, in different ways, to suit the evolving needs of every age. There thus exists an inherent underlying pattern connecting their lives and teachings—most notably, the promise each successive religion of a future messenger who is prophesied to appear during the end of times.

The eschatological prophecies of virtually all major religions have foretold the emergence of a *"World Reformer"*—essentially regarded as the reincarnation or "return" of their religious founders—before the end of the world, who will establish the *"Kingdom of God on Earth"* and usher in an era of peace, justice and prosperity. This messianic *"Promised One"* is known by different names in different religions, being referred to as the *"Everlasting Father"* in Judaism; the *"Spirit of Truth"* in Christianity; the return of Imam Husayn—the *Third Imam*—in Shiite Islam; the return of Prophet Isa (Jesus) in Sunni Islam; Shah Bahram in

Zoroastrianism; "*Kalki*," the final incarnation of Vishnu, in Hinduism; and "*Maitreya*," the Fifth Buddha, in Buddhism.

*Baha'u'llah* considered much of these eschatological prophecies to be metaphoric revelations containing allusions to the future, which should not be viewed literally, but rather symbolically. He thus regarded the prophecy concerning the "end of the world" as a reference to the figurative end of civilization as we know it and its transition to a more evolved, global civilization that has achieved universal consciousness. Similarly, his claims to being the fulfillment of the messianic prophecies of all religions did not constitute the physical return of the Divine messengers and religious founders, but rather, the spiritual return of the same Divine Spirit that manifested through him.

In the public declaration and announcement of his universal mission to the religious leaders of Zoroastrianism, Judaism, Christianity and Islam, *Baha'u'llah* thus symbolically fulfilled his messianic role by paving the way for the promised era of "*the Most Great Peace*" and "*Justice*." In the same way, his proclamations addressed to different world leaders, likewise, served as a symbolic fulfillment of his role as

*"World Reformer,"* functioning *"in accordance with the precepts, of a divinely conceived, a world-unifying, a world-redeeming Order."*

The coming of *Baha'u'llah* is thus regarded by the *Baha'i* community as marking the beginning of a new civilization and the birth of a new stage of evolution for all humanity, as we move toward a new era of peace, justice and harmony. At the same time, *Baha'u'llah* has emphasized the prophetic link as an ongoing *"universal cycle"* that will continue into the future, as many more Divine messengers and *Manifestations* will be sent down at different intervals to future civilizations in order to revive the *"City of God."* He therefore regarded all Manifestations of God, including the ones from the past, as well as those to come, as *"Exponents of both the 'first' and the 'last'"* and has urged his followers to embrace them all as *"one Being,"* who is *"united in their words, speech, and utterance."*

14

# CONCLUSION

Religious intolerance and discrimination has long been a major cause of warfare and bloodshed in the history of our world. Through the course of time, the sacred essence that binds all the major religions of the world together has been corrupted and forgotten under the rise of militant religious fanaticism and fundamentalism, that has gradually torn apart all religious communities, leaving us all divided as a people. It is thus impossible to attain global peace without first addressing our religious differences and engaging in interfaith dialogue.

Despite all their external differences, the *Baha'i* Faith regards the basic purpose of all world religions as inherently the same—which is the establishment of universal order and harmony. The chaos and disorder that prevails in the modern world can therefore be attributed to the failure of religion to serve its true purpose as a social and spiritual force that is necessary for maintaining global peace and stability. *Baha'u'llah* has thus taught that the only means of restoring the *"infallible Balance"* of the world is by collectively embracing the *"changeless Faith of God,"* which is *"eternal in the past,"* and *"eternal in the future."* Ascribing to the principle of *"unity in diversity,"* the *Baha'i* Faith does not regard the plurality of religions as a form of hindrance to order and harmony, but rather, a natural part of the Divine plan, whereby all of humanity is regarded as one and equal, irrespective of the differences that exist between people. As such, it teaches us to accept these differences and respect the beliefs of one another as our own, through mutual tolerance and understanding.

The belief in the oneness of humanity lies at the heart of the *Baha'i* teachings, which emphasize the need to achieve this unity through the single greatest force that connects us all, which is love. This call to unity is beautifully reflected in the following words of *Baha'u'llah*:

> *"So powerful is the light of unity that it can illuminate the whole earth."*

**—Gleanings from the Writings of *Baha'u'llah***

## Core beliefs

The central theme of Bahá'u'lláh's message is that humanity is one single race and that the day has come for humanity's unification into one global society. Bahá'ís believe in:

the oneness of humanity

the common origin and unity of purpose of all world religions

the harmony of science and religion

equality of women and men

the elimination of all forms of prejudice

a spiritual solution to economic problems

the establishment of a world commonwealth of nations

http://www.bahai.us/

# Statement of Faith for the Universal Life Church Monastery of Massachusetts

God or your higher power is holy and calls us to be a holy people.

God or your higher power, who is holy, has abundant and steadfast love for us. God or your higher power 's holy love is revealed to us in the life and teachings, death and resurrection of Jesus Christ, our Savior and Lord. God or your higher power continues to work, giving life, hope and salvation through the indwelling of the Holy Spirit, drawing us into God or your higher powers own holy, loving life. God or your higher power transforms us, delivering us from sin, idolatry, bondage, and self-centeredness to love and serve God or your higher power, others, and to be stewards of creation. Thus, we are renewed in the image of God or your higher power as revealed in Jesus Christ.

Apart from God or your higher power, no one is holy. Holy people are set apart for God or your higher power 's purpose in the world. Empowered by the Holy Spirit, holy people live and love like Jesus Christ. Holiness is both gift and response, renewing and transforming, personal and communal, and ethical. The holy people of God or your higher power follow Jesus Christ in engaging all the cultures of the world and drawing all peoples to God or your higher power.

Holy people are not legalistic or judgmental. They do not pursue an exclusive, private state of being better than others. Holiness is not flawlessness but the fulfillment of God or your higher power 's intention for us. The pursuit of holiness can never cease because love can never be exhausted.

God or your higher power wants us to be, think, speak, and act in the world in a spiritual manner. We invite all to embrace God or your higher power 's call to:

- be filled with all the fullness of God or your higher power;
- live lives that are devout, pure, and reconciled, thereby being an agent of transformation in the world;
- live as a faithful covenant people, building accountable community, growing up, embodying the spirit of God or your higher power 's law in holy love;
- exercise for the common good an effective array of ministries and callings, according to the diversity of the gifts of the Holy Spirit;
- practice compassionate ministries, solidarity with the poor, advocacy for equality, justice, reconciliation, and peace; and
- care for the earth, God or your higher power 's gift in trust to us, working in faith, hope, and confidence for the healing and care of all creation.

By the grace of God or your higher power, let us covenant together to be a holy people.

May this call impel us to rise to this vision of Spiritual mission:

- Preach the transforming message of spirituality
- Teach the principles of love and forgiveness;
- Embody lives that reflect honesty and togetherness;
- Lead in engaging with the cultures of the world; and
- Partner with others to multiply its effect for the reconciliation of all things.

For this we live and labor to the glory of God or your higher power.

---

This book left here by

# *Baha'i* Faith

## *Baha'i* Faith

# *Baha'i* Faith

# *Baha'i* Faith

## *Baha'i* Faith

## *Baha'i* Faith

## *Baha'i* Faith

# *Baha'i* Faith

# *Baha'i* Faith

# *Baha'i* Faith

## *Baha'i* Faith

## *Baha'i* Faith

## *Baha'i* Faith

# *Baha'i* Faith

## *Baha'i* Faith

# *Baha'i* Faith

## *Baha'i* Faith

## *Baha'i* Faith

# *Baha'i* Faith

# *Baha'i* Faith

## *Baha'i* Faith

# *Baha'i* Faith

# *Baha'i* Faith

# *Baha'i* Faith

# *Baha'i* Faith

*Baha'i* Faith

# *Baha'i* Faith

## *Baha'i* Faith

# *Baha'i* Faith

# *Baha'i* Faith

UNIVERSAL LIFE
CHURCH MONASTERY OF
MASSACHUSETTS
We are all people of an equal existence
kindle edition

# FIND US ONLINE

**https://twitter.com/ULCMM**

**https://www.facebook.com/ULCMM**

**http://ulcmm.blogspot.com/**

**http://ministers.themonastery.org/profile/OracleCPam**

**http://ulcmm.com**

For membership inquiries please see us online at http://ulcmm.com

# Formation of our ministry: the Universal Life Church Monastery of Massachusetts

...ordination is a personal calling by God to minister others. I received my calling on several occasions. I didn't understand why at those times. The first was in May 1990. The second time was in May 1998- at this time, I was going through a difficult period in a marriage and prayed for guidance. In May 2004 is was finishing my studies to receive an MBA and felt like my life was not as full as it could be. This last time, in May 2010, I felt as though many people were always turning to me for advice and comfort and I felt at peace with myself and extremely happy. I am ready to spread my knowledge and his word to all that will listen. Please join me.

# ABOUT THE AUTHOR

Oracle Claretta Pam was ordained by the Universal Life Church Monastery headquartered in Seattle, WA. Oracle Pam believes that ultimately we are all one. The path chosen to spirituality is available to all that seek it. She is an Interdenominational Oracle that performs ministerial functions and offers services that include: weddings, civil unions, baptisms, naming ceremonies, life coach services, private ministerial services, house blessings, hospital visitations and funerals. The Oracle is the author of several divinity books and a Guide to Divinity that covers more than 30 religions, belief systems and faiths.

## *Baha'i* Faith

Other forthcoming books available by Oracle Claretta Pam

Agnosticism Atheism Non-Religion
Buddhism
Cao Dai
Catholicism
Christianity
Confucianism
Hinduism
Humanism
Islam
Jainism
Jehovas Witnesses
Juche North Korea
Judaism
Kabbalah
Natural Law
Neopaganism
New Age
Primal Faith
Primal Indigenous
Rastafarianism
Scientology
Shinto
Sikhism
Spiritism
Taoism
Tarahumara Beliefs
Tenrikyo
The Occult
African Traditional - Diasporic
Unificationism
Unitarian Universalism
Zoroastrianism

*Baha'i* Faith

www.ingramcontent.com/pod-product-compliance
Lightning Source LLC
Chambersburg PA
CBHW031251090426
42742CB00007B/403

* 9 7 8 1 4 9 1 3 1 6 2 6 9 *